C000186903

WHISPERING HOPE

PHIL BOSMANS

WHISPERING HOPE

 St Paul Publications

Original titles: *Zomaar voor jou* (10th ed.) © Uitgeverij
Lannoo, Tielt, Belgium 1988
Worte zum Menschsein (6th ed.) © Verlag Herder Freiburg
im Breisgau, West Germany 1986

Translated from the German by Dinah Livingstone
Photographs by G. Zanchin

St Paul Publications
Middlegreen, Slough SL3 6BT, England

English translation copyright © St Paul Publications 1990
Printed in Italy, AGAM Cuneo
ISBN 085439 328 5

St Paul Publications is an activity of the priests and
brothers of the Society of St Paul who proclaim the Gospel
through the media of social communication

Contents

Foreword

Many people have found in Phil Bosmans' books something we all need in our lives: a ray of joy, a flower of happiness, a whisper of hope, the way to an oasis of love. As well as his large books with many pictures, people have often expressed the wish for a handy pocket collection of his finest and most telling remarks. This is what this book offers.

Such a book cannot be read from beginning to end like a novel. This collection of over two hundred texts should be taken like vitamins; it is foolish to overdose. These "heart vitamins" are also most effective when they are taken thoughtfully in small doses.

The texts in this book have a life-long history behind them. They are bound up with the "Association with no Name" (Bond zonder Naam) of Antwerp, Belgium, an open inter-denominational and inter-party movement with a membership of 260,000, founded and inspired by the Catholic priest-monk Phil Bosmans. It is a movement for a more human way of living in the modern world, for putting more heart in human common life. A monthly newsletter, together with widely disseminated cards and posters promote a different lifestyle, a "heart culture". The movement also engages in action for the disadvantaged and prisoners, as well as long-term projects such as the "MIN Hotel" (Hotel for People in Need) in Antwerp, Workplaces for the Handicapped, a Women's House, Sites for Gipsies.

What Phil Bosmans has to say is not worked out at his desk, but comes from experience of meeting countless people and, above all, people in need, unhappy, suffering and despairing people. So it is no accident that his books have been unusually widely published, in large editions and translated into many languages. We hope that this handy collection on "Whispering hope" will help to bring a little more joy into daily life. For, says Phil Bosmans, happy days always come back if you carry the key to them in your pocket.

1

I like you

Lubić ludzi znaczy cieszyć się dobrym
dniami i kosztować przyjemności
z nimi, pomagać im w ciężkich
chwilach
Lubić ludzi znaczy nie szukać
tylko własnego zadowolenia

1. I like you

Szukaj osoby u każdej ludzkiej twarzy [handwritten]

Look for the person in every human face.

Liking people means enjoying good days and having fun with them, offering a helping hand and comfort in bad times.

Liking people means not being self-satisfied but opening your heart and making room in it for others – being clear-eyed and pure-hearted.

I like people – it's my hobby!

Lubię ludzi – to moje hobby! [handwritten]

People fascinate me more and more. People are a daily adventure if you really go along with them.

People are astonishing not only because of what we can see and understand, but also for the mystery we touch in that marvellous

11

package, the body, but which nevertheless eludes us.

There are people who race past us as if impelled by a mysterious power which will not let them rest. People with questioning eyes and tense faces. People who are suffering. People in despair and deeply embittered. People who are no longer capable of feeling any joy. People who are no longer alive. I do not understand them but I do like them. People who need me and people I need, that I cannot do without.

And then there are people whose joy infects you, who cheer you up and help you along. People who like you. The many good simple people hiding great riches in their hearts. Being with people is often a sumptuous feast.

Jeżeli myśli dobrze o mnie

If you think well of me I become better.

Staje się lepszy

No one is as bad as they are in their worst moments. No one is as good as they are at

12

their best. People can all too easily be condemned for life because of one false step. People are usually nailed for wrong behaviour and attitudes. And yet a bad quality does not make a person bad. A bad day does not make a whole life bad.

If I think harm, I will do harm. If I say nasty things about people, they will not become better.

If I think well of someone, I am saying: You do not leave me cold. You mean a lot to me. You are worth taking trouble over. People must like you.

With good people everything turns to good. A good person is a joy to this world. You are a good person!

You are not made for industry and production, counting and consuming. You are made to be human. You are created for the light, for joy, to laugh and sing, to live in love and to cause happiness in people around you.

You are made in the image of a God who is love. You have hands to give, a heart to love with and two arms, which are just the right length to hug someone with.

I believe in the good in people, as I believe in spring, when I see the pussy willow is out.

Angels are human beings through whom light shines. Wherever they are, everything becomes clear and bright. Angels are human beings bringing a bit of joy from heaven with them. Believe me: angels are flesh and blood beings who invisibly keep the world in order. Deep within them you feel something of the mystery of a boundless good that wants to reach human beings at all costs. In them you feel a love that wants to embrace you.

14

You have a problem. You cannot see clear. And as if through an invisible antenna you feel an inspiration, a sort of directive coming to you. It offers help with a useful suggestion or a word of comfort and understanding. "You are an angel", you say. You may say it to a man, a woman, a boy or a girl. Sex and age have nothing to do with it. You are given something good, something glorious. Life becomes bright and the pain has gone.

But angels do not come to order. Sometimes they come quite unexpectedly. Sometimes they are there and hardly noticed. They show you the way and vanish. I have met many angels. Sometimes they stopped in the street, came out of the crowd, reached out a hand, solved a problem and then disappeared into the hurly burly again. Without even saying their name, they melted into the crowd, and did not wait to be thanked.

There are still angels in the world. But there are too few, that is why there is so much darkness and misery. God is looking for angels among people today. But so many people no longer see him, no longer hear him. Their antenna is damaged or broken. They no longer receive or pass on anything.

Well then, you are an angel! You will find plenty of people around you to be an angel for.

Bóg dał każdemu człowiekowi coś co sprawia że inni są szczęśl

God has given each human being something to make others happy with.

I go out in the street. I do not see left-wing people or right-wing people. I just see people.

I struggle to work by bus and train and I do not see left-wing people or right-wing people. I just see people. People in a hurry.

I go to hospital and I do not see left-wing people or right-wing people. I just see people. Sick people, who are in pain.

Why split people up? Why label them? Why paint them this colour or that? Why divide people into good and bad, yellow and

16

red, left and right-wing people? What is the point?

Like people as they are.
There are no others.

Living means living with others. Living with others means having to share with them. They must not suffer through me. I must accept them, welcome them, love them.

If we try to live, love and be happy without others, we are in cloud cuckoo land. We are bound together by thousands of ties. One life depends on another. No life develops without others.

I can only develop through others. I not only need them because they mean so much to me. I also need them because I can do so much for them.

I have eyes to discover others. Ears to hear them with. Feet to walk towards them. Hands to hold them with and a heart to love them with.

17

"I like you." Say it again in words or wordlessly. Say it with a smile, a forgiving gesture, squeeze someone's hand. Speak a word of welcome, say it with a hug, a kiss, a twinkle in your eye. Say it again every day in a thousand small ways: I like you so much.

Tylko szczęśliwa osoba może

Only a happy person can make others happy.

uszczęśliwić innych

My eyes exist to see sunbeams, spring green, the white sparkle of snow, cloud grey, sky blue, for the stars in the night. They exist to see the wonder of all the people around me.

My mouth is to speak with, speak the good word that someone is waiting to hear. My lips are for kissing. My hands can be tender and soft and give bread and comfort to someone who needs it. My feet are for making my way to my neighbour. My heart

18

is for loving, for warmth towards those who are lonely and cold.

Everything has its meaning. So why am I not happy? Are my eyes shut? Is my mouth bitter? Are my hands heartless graspers? Has my heart shrivelled up?

Don't I know I was made for joy?

A happy face and the sun laughs.

So why is it that many people are sullen when the sun is shining and others can whistle in the rain? How come that many people always see mistakes and find fault as soon as they open their eyes? It is because they are wrong about the meaning of life.

They need God. Not a faceless concept but a friend they can trust, a father they can look to. Not a dead distant imaginary being, but the one and only living God who is very near us. If they stay close to God, people get new eyes to look at things

19

with, and wake every morning with a new heart.

Human beings cannot live on earth unless they have a little bit of heaven in mind or heart.

Where there are children, everything becomes fresh and natural, full of colour, warmth and light. Grown-ups do not understand this. They are like that. They are obsessed with earning, always fussing about money. "That is why children must have a lot of patience with grown-ups", says the Little Prince.

When a child makes you glad, you are glad about life.

Treasures lie hidden in many old people. You must know how to discover them. Have

20

time for old people. There is so much talk about the old: their pensions, their housing, their sufferings, great and small, but we do not talk *to* them very much. Why don't you try it for once?

Listen especially to old people who are not worn out by city stress and strain, country people. You will be astonished at their wisdom, their humour, their philosophy, their calm, their assurance, the peace in their hearts.

In every human being lies a deep loneliness. Each of us is unique but also alone. We cannot get into another person's skin. We never think and feel exactly like someone else. Even in the most intimate relationships a painful distance always remains. It can only be bridged by the spirit of love. Loneliness becomes bearable if your spirit seeks contact with others. Without spiritual closeness you will feel desperately alone in your marriage, your family, outside among people in crowded shops and streets. But if you know that somewhere someone is thinking about you and likes you, you will no longer feel lonely.

Being human, a good human being, is the most important thing in the world.

People live longer and longer but not always more happily.

They begin by working in order to live and end up working and forgetting to live. They have understood nothing. They believe that human happiness lies in working hard and earning a lot, in order to have plenty of comfort and free time, to eat well and live long. How can people in this age of so much science be so thick!

Guard against it. You are not a machine, built for some purpose. You are more than your function, more than your post, job, work. First and foremost you are a human being, here to live, laugh and love. To be a good human being is the only really important thing in this world.

When you have grown tired of chasing stars, to bring some light to people in the night, then sit down in silence and listen to the well-spring. When you go deep enough into the heart of things, you get eyes to see invisible things, and ears to hear inaudible things.

est zawsze osoba którą obchodzę

There is someone who always cares for me very much.

Wherever people love, God is at work, God is present. Whoever lives in love, whether a believer or not, lives consciously or unconsciously in the magnetic field of a God who is love.

I feel loved to the tips of my teeth. I'd like to say thank you. I am bursting with gratitude. But tell me whom I should thank. Not a President or a General, not a Professor or Technocrat. I will thank God. I will thank the good God.

He strokes me with a thousand hands. He kisses me with a thousand lips. He feeds me with a thousand fruits. He carries me on a thousand wings. He is my God. I am at home with him. He always likes me.

2

Take time to be happy

You are a miracle living on this earth. You are unique and there is no one like you. Why aren't you amazed and pleased about yourself and all the other people around you? Do you simply take it for granted that you have time to sing and dance and be happy?

Why waste your time in pointless hassling for money? Why load yourself with worries about tomorrow or the day after tomorrow? Why quarrel and get angry? Why rush about being busy or skulk indoors if the sun is shining?

Take time to be happy.
Time is not a fast lane between
cradle and grave.
It is a place to park in the sun.

Today is the day to be happy! You have no other day except today to live, to be happy and contented. If you do not live today, you have lost it.

Don't dampen your spirits with fears and worries about tomorrow. Don't weigh down your heart with all the woes of yesterday. Live for today. Remember what was good about yesterday or think about the good things that may happen tomorrow. But don't get lost in yesterday or tomorrow. Yesterday is over. Tomorrow has not come yet. Today is the only day you have. Make it your best day!

You carry all your past on your back and now do you want to load on all your future as well? That is much too much. Life is given out to you in twenty-four hour portions. So why do you want it all at once? You were not made for that. It will be the end of you.

Do not forget that each day is given to you as an eternity in which to be happy.

Be careful how you wake up in the morning. You are not yet in full control of yourself. It needs an effort to open your eyes. Try to discover what is going on inside you during these first hardly conscious moments of the day. Do you find it glorious to be awake? Are you pleased to be living this day? Are you keen to begin it? Or do you feel a lead weight upon you?

In this first barely waking moment you can discover whether you are happy. This does not mean the all too common "I am all right", "I am not so good". Happiness goes deeper. Can you honestly say yes to your husband, wife, children, the people you meet or live with? Are you happy about the day that willy nilly lies before you? Or have you already secretly capitulated and got up reluctantly?

But be honest. Do not answer too quickly. Do not merely dress yourself up for a part you have decided to play. It is worth taking the trouble to find out whether you are really happy or not. And if the answer is no, why not? No one in the world can change anything at this moment except yourself. There is no one who can live this day in your place.

Accept each day as a gift, a present.
Do not get up too late.
Look in the mirror, smile at yourself
and say: Good morning!
This gets you into practice and then you
can say it to others too.

Yesterday and all the days and years that went before it are over, buried in time. You cannot change anything about them!

Were there troubles? Do not carry them around with you. Because they wear you out day after day and in the end you cannot go on living.

Troubles come but you can get rid of them by putting them in God's hands. There are troubles which you can mend if you honestly forgive. And there are troubles that with all the will in the world you cannot mend. You have to let them be.

Do not begin today with yesterday's troubles.

A happy person brings blessings; an unhappy person makes trouble. A happy person is not dangerous. They have learnt that happiness consists in many little things. They do not insist on it but are glad about what they have.

A happy person does not become obsessed with his/her own problems. They do something for themselves and do not expect everything from others. They do not think of happiness as the big prize in the lottery but know that happiness is like a shadow that follows you unawares.

It is like an answering echo when you give yourself.

Perhaps I seek happiness too far off.
It is like a pair of spectacles.
I cannot see them and yet they are sitting
on my nose!
As near as that.

If we want to be happy, we have to pay a price for it. The price is that we give ourselves, no more, no less.

Giving ourselves has nothing to do with fanaticism or the desire for self-assertion. It is not to do with duty and painful sacrifice. It can only happen freely, joyfully, with love. And then my happiness will be there: as my love's shadow.

Happy people do not pursue happiness
like a butterfly.
They are grateful for what is given them.

You know what bad days are like. Days on which everything goes wrong and every-

32

thing looks black. And the worst of it is you think it will always be like that. Bad days last so long. They are the longest days.

Everybody has bad days. What can you do? On bad days you have to be patient, very patient. Patience is a great virtue and it takes a whole lifetime to learn it. Today everything has to be in such a rush. Every wish must be fulfilled immediately. Just press the button.

But life is not a machine that only churns out good days.

There are good and bad days. Good days pass. You know that and you find it terrible. But bad days also pass! You should remember that and let it be a comfort.

*From time to time you must learn
to fly blind
like pilots in fog.
Blindly let someone else
do the navigating.
Be very patient, even with yourself!*

If you are tired and irritated, if you are fed up with things and can't think what to do about it, if you feel mortally unhappy, then remember the good days of carefree laughter when you were close to someone.

Do not forget the beautiful days! If everything seems dark, and your heart overflows with bitterness, if you feel hopeless, then search your memory for the beautiful days. Days when you were happy and confident. Do not forget your beautiful days! If you forget them they will never come back.

Humour and patience are the camels on which I can travel through the desert.

Laughter is healthy. Easy to say perhaps, but we take too little care of our health in this way. The best health barometer for the individual and the community is joy. Humour is not blind to our own weaknesses and it forgives the weaknesses of others. The only things we usually do not take seriously enough in our lives are joy and humour.

*If you see everything black,
for you morning is sunset!*

Make a point of turning over the page and beginning anew every day. If we do not make a point of this we can let something drag hopelessly on. In the evening we should hand in our page just as it is. Lay it in our Father's hands so that we can begin afresh in the morning.

Each day a new life! Renew yourself and be glad each morning that light comes again. Be happy because your eyes see, your hands feel, your heart beats.

Feel you are alive, that today is the first day of the rest of your life. Look with clear

eyes at people and things. See if you can still
laugh, if you can enjoy simple things like
wayside flowers on your journey.

*Accept what each day brings you:
this day's light, air and life,
laughter and tears, fun
and the miracle of another day.*

3

Joy makes you rich, not possessions

I do not need to possess things in order to enjoy them. There is so much to enjoy if I notice little things and ordinary people. There are so many surprises and so much that is wonderful, waiting for me to discover with my eyes open or shut. There is a memory of paradise lost in everything.

If you can enjoy a flower, a smile, a child's game, you are richer and happier than a millionaire. He may have everything he ever dreamt of but he no longer enjoys it because his own wealth has trapped him. It is not possessions that make you rich, but joy.

Happiness does not come like a cheque or a giro in the post. You can buy lodging and leisure, but nowhere can you ever buy a contented, carefree heart enabling you to enjoy what you have. It is priceless.

39

Advertising's great dogma is that with money you can buy anything. With money you can buy a costly and luxurious house, but not company and warmth. With money you can buy a soft bed, but not sleep. With money you can buy sex, but not friendship. Money can open any door except the door to the heart.

You cannot buy happiness.
Only love gives it freely.

The essential things in life are free. They are given to you for nothing: your mother's womb. A mother who sings to you. Sun and friendship. A place at table and a warm hug. Spring warmth. A child's laughter. Birdsong. The brook's babble. Sap rising in the trees. Sea waves. Day and night. Peace and quiet. The seventh day. Living and dying. Being human on earth.

Look at the lark in the sky, how it sings.
Why?
Because it has no rent to pay!
Look up into the sky and sing because
the sun shines freely on you.

My uncle only saw a little bit of the world. He only had one wife and one house. He worked all day with his hands and everybody was welcome at his table and in his heart. When he was eighty he still enjoyed life as much as when he was twenty. He made me believe in eternal life. If everyone was content with so little there would be enough for everybody.

More than money you need love.
Love is happiness' buying power.

You are more than your money. Your worth cannot be weighed in gold. The more precious things are those you cannot buy with

money: kindness, affection, warmth, good-
will, a warm welcome, pity, recognition,
friendship.

*How I am is infinitely more important
than what I have.*

She was immensely wealthy. But she wanted
to be dead. A house in Hamburg, one in Paris
and one in London. And she wanted to be
dead. She took tablets. The doctors were
able to save her. For two hours I heard her
story. And at the end she cried: "I'd give up
everything, for the sake of a little affection,
a bit of friendship."

Why do so many people get nothing from
life? Because they have no friends. Because
they have no one who is for them. Because
they see no sign that anyone likes them.
Because there are no flowers that bloom for

42

them. Flowers can work miracles! They do not have to be expensive flowers. Common simple flowers; a smile, a hand squeeze, a friendly gesture, a kind word. The simplest flowers come free. Anyone who loses the sense of this richness seeks for substitutes. They throw themselves away on dead things which can never satisfy them. However frenziedly they hunt, they always remain alone in themselves, all alone on the desert island of themselves.

A bit more "we" and a bit less "I".
A bit more kindness and a bit less envy.
A few more flowers in our lifetime and
fewer on our grave.

At the highest standard of living as a human being you may be dying. Perhaps you are already dead? Dead in your greed for money, possessed by your possessions.

Come back to life! Live! Get your head

together and stop this crazy search for more
and more. Protect your heart from the thousand stings of ridiculous desires. Free yourself from things you do not need.

Come back to life! Live! Joy will fill your
spirit. Your eyes will see flowers blooming
again. Your ears will hear birdsong. If you
work with your hands, a bit of bread tastes
wonderful and a glass of water fresh. If the
sun shines you begin dancing and if it rains
you can whistle. And you will feel we are
made for joy.

What is a lost day?
A day during which you have not
laughed!

Laughter frees us. Humour releases ten-
sion. Laughter can save you from false seriousness. Laughter is the best cosmetic for
your outside and the best medicine for your
inside.

44

Humour gives you a feeling for things, for how important they are.

Laughter and humour relieve us. They reduce tensions and tears. They free us from oppressive seriousness and leaden problems, from the suffocating air of the daily grind. Laughter and humour are the best medicine against poisoning of heart and spirit. Laughter and humour open the door to unimagined joy in life.

There has never been so much leisure time, holidays, relaxation. There have never been so many consumer goods, so much alcohol, so many drugs. There has never been such comfortable travel, such well-built houses, such a high standard of living. And there have never been so many unhappy people, so many failed marriages, so many broken families. Without joy life is unlivable, just day following day in boredom and dreariness. Life's deepest meaning is joy.

*Tell yourself: I do not have to have more.
I have enough.*

Lord, free me from seeking things which
cannot satisfy me. Make me free of covetousness, which deceives and makes me
greedier and greedier.

I have two eyes, precious diamonds, and
a mouth to whistle with and health which is
beyond price. Lord, that is enough for me.

I have sun in the sky and a roof over my
head. I have work for my hands. I have a
table to eat at and I have people to love.
Lord, that is enough for me.

4

Reconcile yourself to life

*The sun
does not overlook anyone.
It will shine on you too
unless you skulk
in the shade.*

Human life is strange and incomprehensible. There are days when the sun shines and you don't know why. You are contented. You look on the bright side of life. Work goes with a swing. People are friendly to you. You don't know why. Perhaps you slept well. Perhaps you have found a good friend and feel you are understood and protected. You think: it should stay this way, this peace, this deep joy.

Then suddenly everything changes. It is as if the sun shining too brightly had drawn clouds towards itself. Suddenly sadness falls. Everything looks black. You think other people don't like you any more. You grumble and moan about trivial things. You don't know why. Perhaps you are tired. You just do not know.

Why are things like this? Because human beings are part of nature, with spring and autumn days, warmth of summer and winter cold. Because human beings follow the rhythm of the sea, ebbing and flowing. Because living and dying are the natural rhythms of our existence.

If you understand this then you can press on with courage, confident that after every night comes the morning. If you say yes to this, if you accept life's ups and downs, your life will become deeper and you will know more joy.

Be reconciled to life.
You are stuck in your own skin;
you can't be born again
in someone else's.

If you want to be a little happy, to have a little bit of heaven on earth, you must become reconciled to life, your own life as it is. You must make peace with your work, whatever its limitations, with your own face that you did not choose. You must make peace with the people around you, with their faults and weaknesses. With your husband or wife, even if you know now that you have not met the ideal husband or wife. (They don't exist, anyway.)

You make everything into a problem. The smallest difficulty gets on your nerves. Of course, problems must be solved. If you repress them they fester. But there are many difficulties that are just part of life, marriage, bringing up children, growing old, being with others, work. You must accept these and bravely carry on without making a song and dance about it. If you run away, your problems will catch up with you.

I have met many people. Each of them was different. I have listened to their deepest secrets. None of them had hit the jackpot and come into perfect happiness. They all had something to cope with, some misfortune, burden or hurt. Believers call this a cross. Others say: I have no luck.

Many, in spite of their sufferings, were still, cheerful people. Others broke down if things were difficult. They became too depressed to cope. Often these people had been through similar experiences; only the outcome was very different.

The sun does not overlook anyone.
It will shine on you too unless you skulk in the shade.

"I've had it up to here," he said on the telephone, "I wish I were dead!" Cautiously, I asked his name and what was the matter. "I can't talk," he muttered, "I am here in the office and there are other people…" In the background I heard voices. After a short silence he said, "I am wrecking my own life and others' too. I live too materialistically. I have lost God."

It was two o'clock in the afternoon on a beautiful sunny day, a day to enjoy life. Somewhere in a big office, where a lot of money was made, a man sat at his desk in mortal misery. But I had the feeling he had suddenly woken up – a grace in the middle of this sunny day, the first stirrings of resurrection. This experience was a blessing for him. I do not know his name, but now he may go a different way, perhaps still a long way round, finally find God and feel the sun's warmth again.

You should not be unhappy. If you are unhappy, others will be too. You usually worry too much. Of course everyone sometimes has a reason to be sad. Someone you are fond of suffers severe pain. Perhaps they get ill and will never be better. You suffer with them, rightly so.

But it is not the same thing at all to sour your whole life because of little daily difficulties. For the sake of a rough word, a stain on your clothes, a scratch on your car, for lack of praise you had earned or when you were blamed too harshly. Or because your husband behaves less passionately towards you or your wife no longer looks at you so lovingly. Even small things can sometimes be bitter, but do not make them out to be bigger and worse than they really are. Otherwise you will create an irritable atmosphere which will weigh over you. You should not be unhappy, because if you are you cannot make others happy. And this is your life's task: to make others happy

If your life is difficult, then think of the clown, who is crying inside but who still plays the fiddle to cure others of their heart's pain. The clown's secret lies in a deep, unutterable sadness. The clown knows how painful life is for so many.

You see everything much better with eyes that have wept.

54

Sooner or later you crack your head against the beam and your life becomes a cross. You get ill. You are unlucky. A loved person dies. You have problems at work. You are deceived and left in the lurch by your own husband or wife. You are spied on. Someone has it in for you. You are done down. You cannot cope any more.

The cross is a reality in every human life. But fewer and fewer are up to it. They cannot accept it or bear their own burden. You have no choice! Carry your cross or you will fall under it and be squashed.

You can only carry it when you have understood what it means. The cross brings you back to the truth. The truth that you are a poor, weak, vulnerable human being. It frees you from things that threaten to choke you. It is like an antenna, with which you can obtain news of God. It will not release you from suffering but from suffering's meaninglessness.

You can be human again.

*You cannot banish the cross
from your life.
You must carry it or it will crush you.*

Over the door you close on the past, stands one word: forgiveness. If we think about all the things people do to each other, do together, have to put up with from each other, then we can only find peace through forgiveness. Every word and every gesture offering forgiveness leads to peace.

I know many people and many people's secrets. And I am more and more convinced that no two people are alike.

People are a world to themselves. They live, feel and think and react in terms of their own world, whose deep core I will never know.

That is why there are almost inevitable communication difficulties, frictions, tensions, quarrels between people. Only when

56

I have grasped that the other person is different and am prepared to forgive, is it possible to live together.

The wedding ring is a sign of love and faithfulness. Love and faithfulness can occur in stormy weather.

But days may come when we cannot go on. Stupidity and denial have led to a quarrel. Your house and heart are dark. But there is only one way out back to the light: forgiveness!

It is never too late to make up,
because it is never too late to love
and never too late to be happy.

The sun in the sky of our common life is darkened by clouds of distrust, a fog of insincerity, suspicion, hyprocrisy, or a night of rage and hatred.

57

The sun in our lives is blocked by walls we have built up between people, huge invisible walls in our own house, our own families.

We stubbornly keep the door shut against them because we no longer want to see or hear them.

Reconciliation is the only way to disperse the clouds. It is like morning light gradually breaking through the darkness. Reconciliation is the key which opens locked doors.

You have two hands,
a left hand and a right.
Stretch out one hand leftwards and
the other to the right.
Reconcile people to each other.

I learnt a lot from the sick man. I visited him in hospital. He was half sitting up. His lungs were damaged, because he had worked for many years in a blast furnace, without wearing a mask. He had breathed in flames and now there was oxygen breathing apparatus hanging by his bed. "Oxygen", he said, "is a real boon." And I realized how I enjoyed this boon every day without thinking about it.

Later he even laughed: "I've got a good view here." If he looks out of his window all he can see are the tops of some trees, a couple of clouds and a bit of blue sky. "The people looking after me here are all very kind", he went on to say. And as I was leaving: "Yes, everything will be fine again." And he knows as well as I do that his damaged lungs will never get better.

I learnt a lot from this man. Even in his desperate situation he saw nothing bad. He only noticed the good things. How is that possible? This man can help me to live. Especially on days when I see everything black, although I do not really have anything to complain about.

Day by day, hour by hour, in villages and towns, in a hospital bed or anywhere in the street, there are people who put their heads in their hands and weep about death.

Why is there all this pain? Why are there cripples? Why cancer? Why accidents? Why do people die in spring? Why?

If I think of the dead and about my own death, and about the sufferings of the innocent, I come up against a riddle, a mystery. I can decide to forget about it or stop thinking about it. But as long as I have a mind and heart, I am bound to come back to it. And when the hour comes when I myself have to go into the night of suffering and death, there is nothing else I can do but accept.

I should like to be able to pray when that moment comes, call upon God: "Why have you put out the sun, which you yourself lit?" And I am sure that I will feel things with my heart that I can never explain with my mind.

60

Why not talk about death?
We can learn from it to live
calm and contented lives.

Autumn is beginning. I see it on the trees
and bushes in the garden. I feel it in the air
and in my own limbs. Summer is over. No
plants have grown because it is autumn. But
autumn is beautiful and can be so rich in
colour. Life's final joys are calmer, but also
deeper. So I will let autumn come to me in
peace.

The seed corn does not see the ears of
wheat.

It is the fate of those that give life to die in
doing so. Like the grain of wheat, the seed
potato, the fruit pip and every seed, from
which new life grows. It dies and is forgotten. Likewise good people should know that

61

in everything they bring to life they die and vanish into silence because they have become dispensable. The true art of living lies in being reconciled to this. Such a reconciliation, fully accepting this dying, bears the choicest fruit, the fruit of deep joy in living.

5

Blessed are the non-violent

*The cross is a reality
in every human life.
Carry your cross
or you will fall under it
and be squashed.*

Blessed are the non-violent, who do not hunger for power. They know that people have hands to forgive and not fists to hit with.

Blessed are the non-violent, who resist the orders of technocracy and the demands of an immoderate consumer society.

Blessed are the non-violent, who stand with the weak, with those whom others are prepared to sacrifice. Blessed are they who tirelessly take their stand against the misuse of power.

Blessed are the non-violent, who turn the spiral of violence into a spiral of friendship and love. They are like water in a river, which makes hard stones round and smooth, to roll them along in the stream of goodness. They take over human hearts with gentle force.

In order to become non-violent we must go through the desert to purify our hearts. In the eyes of the powerful and mighty of this world you are the dimwit, the loser.

You must learn to hate violence and love non-violence.

Non-violence means more than not using violence. Non-violence has to do with where we see evil as lying. Whoever sees evil only in systems and structures and in other people is making a fundamental mistake.

Evil is not external but deep in the human heart: when you ignore another person and leave him lying on the ground, when you despise and hate and finally liquidate another human being.

The tactics of non-violence are the tactics of love. It must tear up evil by the roots.

There is evil in the world. Evil is in human hearts. It gives the will the energy to hate, to destroy and kill. It gives muscles the power to use weapons, throw bombs, fire off rockets.

There is good in the world. The good is like a small seed in human hearts. It grows in silence. It does not come with violence. It slowly ripens, if it gets a little warmth from other human beings. There is a lot of good seed. But in a cold world it cannot grow and blossom and bear fruit.

We must learn to fight evil,
without doing evil to anyone.

The world is locked into a vicious circle. Evil calls to evil. Violence generates violence. One injustice follows another. If someone strikes us, we do not try to forgive them but strike back. We are caught up in the same vicious circle.

It is incredible. Suddenly a human face entered history and broke through the vicious circle and showed a new way out, the way of forgiveness. Jesus met enemies with words of forgiveness. His life and death revolutionized the world and offers each generation the choice: violence or non-violence! Forgiveness or revenge!

You cannot banish darkness
with darkness.
Only with light.
You cannot heal hatred with hatred.
Only with love.

If I make an enemy I can no longer talk to him, eat with him, live with him, work with him, be with him. If I make an enemy the only thing I can do is fight him.

You can crack nuts but not people!

68

People are killed for money. People are thrust aside for the sake of a career. People are blackened through jealousy. People are crushed for the sake of competition. Go up to people with a kindly outstretched hand. It is not hard to break people. Offer the bread of kindness. Be a refuge, a haven, an oasis.

I want to change the world
but not through violence.
I value people too much.

The violent destroy everything. The violent are bulldozers. They flatten everything in their path. They squash things that are tender and weak and easy to harm. Every day people are sacrificed to other people. The shadow of violence lies over human happiness. But violence cannot be healed by violence. We must abandon the way of violence, the way of bloodshed and tears, the way of death, the old way pursued by

69

generations, believing in force, possession and that might is right.

We must go a new way, the way through darkness to light, the long way of love, so that joy can shine in our lives like a bright rainbow in the sky of our village that is called earth.

The first blow is usually a word.

Be careful how you speak. Words are powerful weapons that can do a lot of harm. A harsh, poisonous, lying word can cut deep and hurt for a long time. Let your words be kind.

If your heart is an oasis for others, then your words will be like water, to make the desert bloom. Speech is a wonderful gift given to us by God so that we can talk to each other, work and live together. Words should not be weapons to fight each other with.

70

Let God be in your speech then your words will shine with life and love.

Life is much too short
and our world far too small
to turn it into a battle-field.

The way we live together is cold and hard. Our speech is violent and threatening. Protests. Orders. Tyranny. The world needs warmth, kindness, tenderness. You will become tender when you know how fragile things are and how lonely people are.

Be gentle and kind!
Don't leave people out in the cold.

Non-violence means more than just being nice to others. Non-violence means standing against all injustice, exploitation and corruption. Non-violence is not just the refusal to kill or torture others, but also a refusal to exploit another human being for profit. Non-violence means fighting at the risk of your own life for the rights of minorities, the rights of the poor and powerless; transforming through non-violent actions all inhuman, repressive social structures into structures with a human face.

Share your bread and it tastes better.
Share your happiness and it grows.

We all know that millions of human beings are suffering from hunger. They cannot work because they have nothing to eat. They are ill because they have nothing to eat. They die young because they have nothing to eat.

What do we do, we who have laden tables and soft beds? Have we done anything about the twentieth century's greatest scandal? Do we feel any sympathy? Do we talk about it? Do we shift the blame onto others?

Being shocked does not help. Sympathy does not help. Talking about it does not help. Shifting the blame onto others is running away. We must share!

I often hear people saying: "Stop bothering us with your development aid." It was at an international conference in Paris. A black teacher came forward, waited till the room was completely silent and then he shouted: "Leave us alone with your development aid. This aid has not helped us. If you want to help us then put yourselves in our shoes and go our way. Drink from the same cup as we do and then you will see that we cannot use your approach to life."

If we want to survive we must live differently. We must hold other values more important than money and comfort and develop a new lifestyle. We will only share in fellowship with others if we can live in fellowship.

Put all the weapons in the world in the hands of Francis of Assisi and you can sleep soundly.

In times of war people can give up anything, they are prepared for any sacrifice. They suffer deprivations and hunger. They give their money and their lives. And the result? Millions of fellow human beings are killed. Thousands of towns and villages are destroyed. Why does war give people so much strength to suffer? Why does not peace give people the power to deny themselves anything?

6

Only love makes you human

Love is not a luxury for kind-hearted and gentle souls. Love is not like extra summer blossoms that some get and others do not, without either being able to do anything about it. Love is not to be confused with sentimentality or almsgiving, with works of charity and mercy. Love has nothing to do with solidarity within powerful groups and parties, in which you only help yourself and others like you.

Love means loving people, not systems, parties, structures. It means loving people, not humanity in the abstract. It means loving particular people as they are around you and people that come into your living room on the television, because they are hungry or have suffered catastrophe, are oppressed, exploited and persecuted. Love requires things that are no longer in fashion: living simply, self-denial, friendship, kindness, faithfulness. Love goes much deeper than sharing wealth and welfare. In love's economy you have to give more than you possess. You have to give yourself.

If I do not have love, then what do I have? Money? Enjoyment? Superfluity? What shall I do with it? What does it make me? Nothing!

What am I without love?
A big zero!

If you set foot on the moon but had no love, you would have no idea of the sun. If you searched out all the secrets of Mars and had no love, no star would shine in your eyes. If you possessed all the money in the world but had no love, your heart would be a stone. If you heard your name spoken in every language on earth but had no love, you would be dead to all others. If you have no love, you are dead.

Y ou may be the poorest, weakest and most sinful of human beings. If you have love, you can live. You may be laid low by sickness, misfortune and loss. If you have love, you can stand. You may not have a large house, just a roof over your head. If you have love, you are at home. You may have no possessions and no money in the bank. If you have love, you have God in your heart.

Love is like the sun.
Whoever has it may lack many things.
Whoever lacks love lacks everything.

F or many the sun is the most familiar thing in the world. It works miracles day after day. It makes light and fire – for me. It shines through clouds in order to see me, to say good day to me.

At night the sun is at the other end of the earth to give its light to the people there. If I take away the sun it is dark and cold.

That is how it is with love. If love rises in my life, then light comes and it is warm. If I have love, I may lack many things. If love sets in my life then the shadows increase. It becomes dark and cold.

A flower needs sunshine
to become a flower.
A human being needs love
to become human.

A little love can be like a drop of water, giving a flower the power to stand upright again.

A little love can heal a human being. Healing a human being means helping him to find his lost courage again.

If I am really going to love, I must care about human beings. I must be attentive,

sympathetic and sensitive. First towards the people close to me, who are entrusted to my care, those I live with or work with every day and who are part of my life.

Caring about others connects me with them and tears me out of my own narrow self.

It is urgently necessary so that I do not go circling endlessly round myself.

My fellow human beings want my love, need my recognition, friendship. I can help them every day anew, with a friendly glance, a kind word, a sensitive hand. My fellow human beings do not live over the mountains or across the sea. They live here. Why do I seek so far away?

Only water can change a desert.
Water is life.
Love is living water.

Our society has heart disease. It needs the serum of love.

In our artificial world something is wrong. Something is forgotten, something fundamental and irreplaceable. We have made social laws, organized social services with bureaucracies but forgotten one thing, that all this is meaningless if behind the shutters, desks and mountains of paperwork there is no human heart. We have no lack of information, knowledge and ability but a great lack of love.

Love is the foundation of all happy common life. If there is room for the heart, then small weak human beings are back at the centre wherever human beings live and work together. The human person is back in the centre of social, political and economic life.

You are only free if you love. Absolute freedom is the freedom of the strongest, the law of the jungle. Not freedom but love is the highest human value, if you are no longer bound up in your own ego and self-ishness. Freedom can only flow in the stream of love.

Slight love sees big faults everywhere.

Love is always a little blind to other people's mistakes. If love and friendship wither, then this blind sympathy is also lost. Then we look on the bad side, and finally only see faults and blemishes, weakness and fail-ures... the bad things.

I often wonder why human beings do not manage to love. Why is it difficult living together every day? I think it is because we deceive ourselves. We intend to love

83

others but really we love ourselves, our own ego.

We ask too much of others. The other person should be friendly. The other person should understand me. The other person should admire me, carry me, go through fire for me. He must not get in bad moods or have any weak points. And woe betide him if he criticizes me. The smallest disappointment and I am cut to the heart.

We think too little about what we owe others, what we can give, what we can do for them. Do not be too quick to say: "You don't love me", as long as you yourself have not given everything.

You can only hold on to people through love. Otherwise you repel them.

People are not just put on earth, thrown onto our planet. People are entrusted to other people. The first and most fundamental right is the right to love. Every human being that comes into the world has an inalienable right to a father and a mother, the right to a home, right to human warmth, right to shelter.

The process of becoming a human being begins in our mother's womb. Only in the shelter of love can a human being develop humanly.

When love makes people human, heaven comes upon earth.

A bird thrown out of its nest dies. A child that is not hugged, grows cold. In order to become human, people need warmth and a lot of love. Loving people because they are so "lovable" ends in fiasco.

People are not always so lovable that we like them just as they are. Forgiving our enemies and loving our opponents, returning good for evil, is superhuman if there is no deeper reason for it.

God is love. This is the astonishing message in the new book for our time, in the old Gospel that describes God's humanity. It is the most human and most divine message of all time. The opposite of all past ideologies.

The Gospel is not a doctrine. The Gospel is life.

God's love has become visible and touchable in a human body, a human heart, the person of Jesus of Nazareth. God became human so that human beings loving one another could become human.

In Jesus the source of kindness is revealed. In him God chose humanity, God put humanity at the centre.

In Jesus God is on the side of the poor, the weak, the powerless. In him God's love has become human.

The Gospel of love is something crazy. People who go for this love abandon their position of power, give up seeking superiority and take the last place, so as to serve others.

The Gospel is the message of a love that hurts, that is signed with the craziness of the cross.

God is present in every human being who likes you, who finds you worth taking trouble over, who goes with you and stays with you, when evening comes.

God is looking at you through the loving eyes of every human being who understands you. He is present in every kind word that comforts and supports you. He is in the hand clasping your shoulder to give you courage and lovingly putting you right when you are going the wrong way.

God is present in the mouth that kisses you. It is his warmth you feel when you are hugged. Where love dwells in human hearts people can speak meaningfully about God and understand one another.

*Love is not experience of people.
It is experience of God.*

7

Make friends with nature

Everything has been given to us human beings. All life has been entrusted to us. The first man could have been a gardener in a paradise that bloomed freely for him. But we have turned our hands into giant grabbers and our feet into giant shovels, so that everywhere our monuments arise out of steel and concrete to our own honour and glory. Now many sit there dead among a thousand dead things, desperately looking for a life pill.

We are the cause
of environmental pollution:
the poisoning of our spirit and
the meanness of our souls.

Weep mother earth in grief
for what you delivered!

You kept life snug and warm in your womb. You were fruitful in a thousand plants. Millions of animals played upon you, in the green grass and the ocean depths. Countless birds, butterflies and insects play in your woods and meadows and dance in the air.

Weep mother earth in sorrow
for the disgrace human beings
have brought upon you!

They have plundered your raw materials that need millions of years to form in your womb. In greedy haste they have robbed you of your riches and squandered the patrimony of their children and children's children.

Weep mother earth for sheer grief
at the crimes
the human race has committed!

Our earth is a wonderful place to live. Humanity is its ruler but must not be its robber. There is a close mysterious bond between all things in the whole of creation. Human beings, animals, trees breathe the same air, live from the same sun and are nourished by the same fruits of the earth. Every attack on nature is an attack on humanity itself. Ill-treating animals, destroying animal species, is a crime against humanity. What happens to animals today can happen to humans tomorrow.

Whoever disturbs earth's balance of nature turns our home planet into a wilderness.

Even though animals cannot speak, they cry for their rights in all languages.

Anyone who can talk to a tree
does not need a psychiatrist.
Most people think the opposite.

I thought I knew them, the apple tree and the cherry tree, until one day I saw the miracle.

They stood with their roots in the same earth, lifted their branches into the same air, sun and rain. And the apple tree made apples and the cherry tree ten yards away made cherries. Perfectly normal, people said. But I did not trust my eyes. What they took out of the same soil, the same air, sun and rain, made one tree produce cherries and the other nearby produce apples. And they are quite different in shape, colour, smell and taste. I had never seen such a miracle before.

If you want to make friends with a tree, then look carefully at what it is showing you. You will see its wealth and its poverty, its growth and blooming in spring, its fruits in summer, its dying in autumn and death in winter. If you want to make friends with a tree then never tear at its roots or it will die forever.

The same goes for human beings.

How do leaves come on the tree? Because deep down in the earth large and tiny roots seek nourishment. Through them the tree can grow and become big.

*Flowers bloom even when no one
is looking at them.
Trees bear fruit
without asking who eats it.*

The calendar full of dates, the mad dash from one appointment to the next. Does life make you tired with a narrow round of too many trivia?

Go into the woods. It is spring there. The flowers are waiting for you. Beautiful flowers that live silently on the sap that rises to their furthest tips. Birds sing there for you. Go into the woods. Lie down under a tree, chew a blade of grass and enjoy doing sweet nothing. Thoughts and dreams will come freely. Your indoor problems will recede.

Enormous love is built into nature. You only need to look at a flower quietly.

Dear onion, how do you know it is spring? A year ago I brought you in and put you on the shelf in the shadow of a book. I did nothing to you, absolutely nothing. I just waited. Perhaps for the time when I felt like eating you…

You lay there for a whole year. And now you suddenly sprout. You saw no sunshine. You were given no water. I only looked at you. Now suddenly you come out to tell me: spring is here.

Who wrote that in your heart? I'll thank the Invisible, who programmed you, who enabled you to live so intensely in complete silence. A miracle! Maybe we can analyse it scientifically in every detail, but that does not take away the miracle, it does not take away the message you bring me: it is spring.

A mystery of love is built into nature. I find
that fantastic. My heart beats over a hundred
thousand times a day, freely. It is unbeliev-
able. Every day I breathe twenty thousand
times, and for the hundred and thirty-seven
cubic metres of air I need I am charged
nothing.

I sowed radishes, tiny little seeds. I could
hardly hold them in my fingers. I went to
sleep, I got up. It rained, the sun shone. I did
my work and forgot about the radishes.

But for three weeks someone had to do
with them. He lovingly welcomed the radishes into the earth's womb and fed them.
Now they were growing fat. They were five
hundred times fatter than the seeds I had
sown in the earth. For weeks we were able
to enjoy delicious fresh radishes.

A plant is more than a chemical organism.
It goes beyond all the chemical structures

and laboratories in the world. It carries out the most complicated chemical reactions and we still do not know how it does so.

I have met many people in my life. I have sometimes wondered whether I could find someone capable of making me a blade of grass. I found plenty of people who could tell me how a blade of grass came about, how it is put together, and also people who could copy a blade of grass but it was always only a dead copy.

Blades of grass do not bring the spring. But they have so much power that they can break through dead asphalt. I cannot alter a desert in one day. But I can begin with an oasis.

We must adopt new ways:
the way of seeds.

Every seed is a rich promise. It carries a whole world inside it. It carries the promise of ripening wheat in golden fields: barns full of wheat, bread for us.

A seed is like a night prayer. It surrenders itself to mother earth's mysterious power, to die in a silent embrace, then to burst out and bear fruit in a new life.

The seed. The great mystery of living and dying, silence, simplicity, hiddenness. It gives itself up to earth's darkness. It feels the sun's warmth. It drinks the blessed rain. The seed corn does not see the ripe wheat but it believes in it. The seed's way is the way for every human being to maturity and fruitfulness.

Had you realized that everything in nature pushes towards light? The smallest seed grows out of the earth's darkness towards light. Every tree, however thick the forest, stretches up its branches towards the light. Every flower opens its petals to the sun.

But human beings have turned away from the light. They have grown grey with grey materialism. Matter rules human beings to their depths. It is a sick worship of money and possessions, power and wealth.

The spirit is oppressed, we think and feel wrong, our behaviour is corrupt. This is the worst harm the modern, highly industrialized world has done us. When the spirit is oppressed, the heart grows hard and there is savage conflict in society. Our life withers at the root. Many people lose hope and are impelled by dark forces to throw their lives away.

Everything that lives seeks light.
Dying things make for the dark.
Why do so many people today live
in darkness?

Once upon a time there were two bees who sat at the entrance to their hive in the sunshine. A heavy storm had been raging for a long time, creating havoc and destroying flowers. "Where can I fly now?" complained the first bee. "Everything is destroyed. What can I do about it?" And it remained where it was, sad. "Flowers are stronger than the storm," said the other bee. "There must still be flowers somewhere, and they need us, they need us to visit them. I am off." Away it flew.

Some years ago a young man painted a picture for me. As if in a vision he had painted the end of our planet. A terrifying picture. In the distance the cities of the rich were burning.

A gaping chasm had split the earth and four lean grim men were carrying a coffin towards it, out of the city of the rich and past the hovels of the poor. To the right a woman cowering on the ground, with her arm stumps raised to heaven, wept in despair. In the centre stood the illusion of hope, a flower with a big chunk cut out of its stalk. The last flower was dying.

We stare at the ruins of our world. But if our hearts can still believe in light and love between human beings, then the flower will heal. The missing piece of the stalk will grow back. Where one flower can bloom, one day a thousand flowers will grow.

stalk - kodyga

8

The dream of a new world

When human lights go out and the noise of the world is hushed, we see the stars, we hear silence again. There are stars in the night that we have never seen. If it gets even darker they shine. You are looking up again. Hope returns because you can see further.

When a crisis has darkened everything, stars will be kindled by the children of light.

There are people who bring light to others, and new life. These are people who free themselves from covetousness and hate. People who no longer believe in weapons. People who are content with little and have time for things that do not bring in money. People who do not need a palace to enjoy living, who do not need a fat wallet to have good parties together. People who see flowers, hear birds singing, who can play like children and fall asleep in a chair. Kind people who are full of light.

We need a new spring, a spring of the heart and spirit. For the girl who wrote to me she was as good as dead, her life was so meaningless. For the man no longer at peace with his wife and children. For the woman who contemplates suicide, because there is no one who needs her, no one to live for. For the many who feel no joy and so try to buy pleasure instead, like petrol for the car.

We are sated with good living, which lets us down. We need to rise again. With a new spirit and a new heart. Not with the help of pills and tablets but through the mysterious powers that slumber deep in every human heart.

If you are dead to every joy and every love and happiness, if you can no longer believe in yourself and human beings, then

106

try for once to get rid of all that is ugly, poisonous, dark and miserable in a clean sweep. Get up out of the darkness of your discouragement and weariness to a new morning full of sunshine, birds and flowers. Wake up from the hibernation of your dreary existence to a new spring. Arise! God has written resurrection into every leaf of every tree. So your poor human heart must also have that power.

We are all in the same boat.
We must all pull together.

All human beings pulling together in the same boat… the sun dancing in the sky, fish leaping in the sea. A beautiful dream.

All human beings together in the same world boat. Weak and strong, black and white, big and small, poor and rich: people travelling together. No one will be thrown overboard. No stowaways. No one fights

107

over the command bridge. On board this ship everyone is secure and protected. A beautiful dream!

Why do I have to wake up and see a black rudderless ship, sailing with difficulty? Why do I hear those despairing cries?

What does not come from the heart cannot reach another heart.

Look at your own face in the mirror. You live behind it. Your face is a mirror of your inside. If your face does not smile any more then something is wrong inside. Your heart is sick. A cold face comes from a cold heart. People with sour faces make life sour.

Heal your heart. Fetch a smile out of it, in the street, at the booking office, at work, at home. Smile just for the sake of it.

You think with your heart more than with your mind. You see people and things with your heart. You see everything with your heart. Your relationship to your surroundings is ruled by your heart. What your heart wants is what you will pursue with all your mind and with all your strength. Ideas, ideology, politics: the heart chooses what you fight for. The heart makes the mind clear or makes it dark. The heart's true measure is called love.

A single word which has only to enter your heart to transform it – one word can become all this: a birth, a bit of bread for a new beginning, a star falling from heaven.

You know how little, poor and lonely human beings are, how sensitive and vulnerable. You know there are tears and no one to comfort them. You know there is hardly any greater sadness than that felt by a heart whom no one understands. You know that for many people life is an unbearable pain.

109

Be gentle! Do your best to understand people and help them. Enter into their suffering and loneliness. Come down from your peak of self-satisfaction into the valley of humanity, to the people below needing help or shelter. Do not be hard and do not be hard in your judgement.

Everyone who removes an obstacle so that people can go forward and go on living does a great deal more than one who climbs up onto the obstacle and trumpets that it is there, that it should not be there, that it must finally be got rid of. But he himself does nothing and blames others for the obstacle still being there.

If I want to improve the world,
I should start with myself!
We are not alone in the wilderness
if we can believe in the oasis.

110

I believe there will be a new spring throughout the world if every soldier, wherever he is fighting, lays down his weapons and calls out to his visible or invisible enemy: "Man, I like you. I can't kill you. I can't do you harm."

I believe in a sea of new possibilities if the rich grow ashamed of their wealth, lay down their power and possessions, go to the poor and say: "I like you. Forgive me! I took too much for myself. I want to sit down at your table with food on it for us to share, and peace-flowers in the sun."

I believe in the miracle that in every house, in every street, every town, one person says to another: "I like you. I will rid my mouth of all its bitter words, fill my heart with kindness and my hands with gifts of friendship."

I wish you the courage of the morning sun, which rises day after day over this world and its pain.

111

A new time is coming. Birth is bound up with pain, sometimes a lot of pain, labour pains. We need people who know where the hurt is, who know the reasons for the pain, who are both competent and gentle.

We need people like Francis – a poor man of God without arrogance or ambition, a simple man with the healing power of poverty, a little brother full of joy, who turns to everyone with unstinting love.

9

Simply be human

Simply be human, live simply. Look up at the sky, see the sun, gaze at the flowers and the stars at night. Watch children laughing and playing; do things that bring joy; daydream, let your imagination play, be contented. Life is a feast.

Let's make every year People Year, just People. Not Academics' Year, Workers' Year, Politicians' year, Astronauts' or Patriots' Year. Not Personnel Administration, Data Processing or Psychic Therapy Year. Not Women's Year, Men's Year or Children's Year. Just People Year, quite ordinary people on quite ordinary days under the ordinary sun.

Enjoy small things, then wherever you are you can always be a little happy.

Happiness – I have searched deep for its cause and found it. It does not lie in money or possessions or luxury; it does not lie in leisure or business, not in performance or consumption. In happy people I have always found the reason was deep security, spontaneous joy in small things and a great simplicity.

Letters, phone calls, conversations show me the jungle where human beings humiliate each other, hurt each other and bring despair.

Here the inhuman instincts triumph: greed, selfishness, abuse of power. When I am with people who have been sacrificed, people who are at the end of their tether and want to make an end to their life, I feel like shrieking into this jungle: Go back! Go back to the simple life, to the simple things in life! Go back to kindness, friendship, contentment.

*Simple people: the only lungs
through which our world can still
breathe.*

Simple people – wonderful people. People
who without making any fuss about it pour
a stream of love upon the world. They are
oases in our desert, they are stars in our
night.

To be loved. A wonderful feeling. Spring in
your heart. Everything becomes different,
everything gains colour. If you are loved,
everything looks rosy and sunny, because
you have become blind in one eye, the eye
that sees the bad, the ugly side of life.

There are many ways of loving, but one
way is particularly important for us in our
confusing complicated society: loving in
ordinary everyday things. Rediscover the
simple things: friendship, a few flowers for
a sick person, an open door, a hospitable

table; eating an egg or a herring, lying back on a garden lounger and staring into the sky; holding hands, a smile, the silence in a church; a child's painting; a flower in bloom, birds twittering, a poplar avenue, a stream, a mountain, a cow… Life is a feast if you can enjoy the simple everyday things.

Work with your hands,
the most natural and effective way
to spiritual healing.

Work with your hands. Wander about in the country. Eat when you are hungry. Sleep when you are tired. Talk to trees and worms. Make music for birds and fishes in a stream. The miracles around you will give you new eyes. You will need less but enjoy it more and with more awareness. Enjoyment is a blessing. Being content with little and enjoying a great deal is the art of happiness practised by the truly free.

When plants feel the sun in the morning, they begin to live. If people feel a human heart in the morning, they come to life.

Under your skin there is an angel, waiting with a message of kindness and love for human beings on earth. Let the angel speak in what you do.

With every good person living in the world a sun rises

A good person is like a little light wandering through the night of our world and re-kindling dead stars on its way.

The goodness that people show others in friendship and love is worth far more than efficiency and competition. It cannot be measured, it cannot be pinned down in statistics. It lies deeper, it is like an invisible warm Gulf Stream, felt on the coasts of a world in which we have too long been chilled by the coldness among people.

Living means embracing people and things and letting them go again, so that they may flourish and bloom in God's sight.

Living means being grateful for the light and love, warmth and tenderness which are given so simply in people and things. Living means seeing everything as God's gift, possessing nothing and no one, and rejoicing over every star that falls from heaven.

A friend in your life is like bread and wine.

A friend. A person who goes with you for a while along the same road. Two friends do not look at each other as much as they both look forward. They do not seek each other; they seek together what each needs. Anyone who demands everything from friendship falls into jealousy and isolation. A true friend helps you to get on with your own life and do what you want to do. So he will never

120

hold you back or drag you away from the right road in your own life. Real friends do not let you down either on good or bad days. They stay near in joy and pain, in power and weakness. We have to hide many things from outsiders because the outside world will not tolerate weakness. But when friends are close it is possible for us to be honest and open.

You can endure anything and get through it if you have a friend at your side. Even if there is nothing he can do except say a word or hold your hand.

A friend in your life is the greatest comfort in all need.

In a friend's true human kindness you feel God's own kindness.

Do not be discouraged. Become a good human being then the little bit of world in which you live will become a better bit.

You have hands to give with.
You laugh and like people.
You are simply human,
that is why you are great.

To be happy in this world full of surfeit and arrogance we need its simplicity. Get up each morning and say: "Good morning! I am happy to be here, my house has a roof, the sun is up, I like the people around me. I can create and do not need a monster car or nightmare fur coat in order to go on my way!"

A good person is like a flower that blooms all day in the sun. If a butterfly perches on it, with all the beauty of its petals it says, "Thank you".

If you only live on the surface, if you are only interested in your outside, your appear-

122

ance, your make-up, being in fashion, then your happiness will be at the mercy of fashion, swinging on a pendulum: happy today, unhappy tomorrow, in fashion today, in despair tomorrow.

Go inside yourself. Make something of yourself inside, where your heart is. There dwell the dispositions and driving forces that can bring you to joy or grief.

If you have five minutes, do you know what you should do? Reflect a little!

Make some peace and quiet. Turn off the radio, cassette player or television; put away the newspaper.

Make some space for silence, fill yourself with silence and listen to your own heart beat.

If you want to warm the world
you must have a big fire inside yourself.

You can't live without comfort. But comfort is not alcohol, sleeping pills, drugs. These only deceive and make things worse. Comfort is not a flood of words. Comfort is like a soothing ointment on a painful wound. Comfort is like an unhoped-for oasis in a pitiless desert. Comfort is like a gentle hand on your head, helping you to rest. Comfort is like a kind face looking at you, someone who understands your tears, listens to your pain, who stays with you in your agony and despair and points you towards a couple of stars.

Let's be an oasis,
where we can be enthusiastic about life,
every life,
even the life that gives a lot of trouble.

We have turned the world into a dust bowl full of atomic explosives with 1,500,000 times the explosive power of Hiroshima.

We have poisoned the world, dead fish in dead waters, dying trees in dying forests. We have plundered the world, squandering its raw materials. The rich countries grab all its foodstuffs for themselves and in poor countries there is bitter want.

The world is a desert. Who will save it? Not generals, not politicians, not technocrats! The "world desert" can only be saved by "oasis people". People with a new awareness of the values we have been deprived of by technical and scientific progress. Not other people but changed people. People who live more simply, more contentedly and more humanly. In the middle of the desert the oasis grows. Oasis people do not make revolution. Oasis people are the revolution.

If a flower can bloom again, then one day a thousand flowers will bloom.

Personal notes

Personal notes

Personal notes